Working in the United States.
A comprehensive guide.

Arthur Crandon LL.B (Hons.) M.A.

Working in the US

Copyright Arthur Crandon 2024

All rights reserved. No part of this book may be reproduced, stored in a retrieval system, or transmitted in any form or by any means—electronic, mechanical, photocopying, recording, or otherwise—without the prior written permission of the publisher, except for brief quotations in critical reviews or articles.
This is a work of fiction. Names, characters, places, and incidents are either the product of the author's imagination or used fictitiously. Any resemblance to actual persons, living or dead, events, or locales is entirely coincidental.

ISBN: 9798336602678

Cover design by Lynnie Ceniza
Interior design and formatting by Lynnie Ceniza
Published by Arthur Crandon Publishing
Visit our website: Arthurcrandon.co.uk

DISCLAIMER
The information provided in this book is for general informational purposes only. It does not constitute legal, financial, or professional advice. While every effort has been made to ensure accuracy, the author and publisher assume no responsibility for errors or omissions. Readers should consult with appropriate professionals for specific advice tailored to their individual circumstances.
First Edition: August 2024

CONTENTS

1	Understanding Visa Requirements	1
2	Finding a job in the U.S.	9
3	Preparing your application	15
4	Visa Application Process	21
5	Work Culture	27
6	Legal and Financial	33
7	Settling in the U.S.	39

1 UNDERSTANDING VISA REQUIREMENTS

To work in the United States, you will need a visa that allows employment. There are two main types of visas for this purpose:

Nonimmigrant Visas: These are temporary visas for individuals who plan to work in the U.S. for a specific period. Common types include:

- **H-1B Visa**: For specialty occupations requiring a higher education degree. This visa is popular among professionals in fields such as IT, engineering, and healthcare. The employer must demonstrate that the job requires a specialized knowledge and that the employee has the necessary qualifications.

- **L-1 Visa**: For intra-company transferees who work in managerial positions or have specialized knowledge. This visa allows companies to transfer employees from their foreign offices to their U.S. offices.

- **O-1 Visa**: For individuals with extraordinary ability or achievement in fields such as science, arts, education, business, or athletics. Applicants must provide evidence of their extraordinary abilities, such as awards, publications, or significant contributions to their field.

- **E-2 Visa**: For investors and treaty traders from countries with which the U.S. maintains a treaty of commerce and navigation. Applicants must invest a substantial amount of capital in a U.S. business and demonstrate that they will develop and direct the enterprise.

- **J-1 Visa**: For exchange visitors participating in programs that promote cultural exchange, such as research scholars, professors, and medical trainees. This visa is often used for internships, training programs, and educational exchanges.

Immigrant Visas: These are for individuals who intend to live and work permanently in the U.S. Employment-based immigrant visas include:

- **EB-1**: For individuals with extraordinary abilities, outstanding professors, and researchers, or multinational executives and managers. Applicants must provide evidence of their extraordinary abilities or achievements, such as major awards or significant contributions to their field.

- **EB-2**: For professionals with advanced degrees or exceptional abilities in the sciences, arts, or business. Applicants must have a job offer and an approved labor certification, unless they qualify for a National Interest Waiver.

- **EB-3**: For skilled workers, professionals, and other workers. This category includes jobs that require at least two years of training or experience, as well as positions that require a bachelor's degree.

- **EB-4**: For special immigrants, including religious workers, certain international organization employees, and other specific groups. Each subcategory has its own eligibility requirements and application process.

- **EB-5**: For investors who invest a significant amount of capital (typically $1 million, or $500,000 in targeted employment areas) in a U.S. business that creates at least 10 full-time jobs for U.S. workers. This visa is designed to stimulate economic growth through foreign investment.

Application Process for Nonimmigrant Visas

1. **Job Offer**: Secure a job offer from a U.S. employer willing to sponsor your visa.

2. **Petition Filing**: The employer files a petition with the U.S. Citizenship and Immigration Services (USCIS) on your behalf. For example, Form I-129 for H-1B, L-1, and O-1 visas.

3. **Petition Approval**: Once the petition is approved, you can apply for a visa at a U.S. embassy or consulate in your home country.

4. **Visa Interview**: Attend a visa interview

where you will need to provide documentation and answer questions about your employment and background.

5. **Visa Issuance**: If approved, you will receive your visa and can make travel arrangements to the U.S.

Application Process for Immigrant Visas

1. **Labor Certification**: For most employment-based immigrant visas, the employer must obtain a labor certification from the U.S. Department of Labor, demonstrating that there are no qualified U.S. workers available for the position.

2. **Petition Filing**: The employer files a petition with USCIS on your behalf. For example, Form I-140 for EB-1, EB-2, and EB-3 visas.

3. **Petition Approval**: Once the petition is approved, you can apply for an immigrant visa at a U.S. embassy or consulate in your home country.

4. **Visa Interview**: Attend a visa interview

where you will need to provide documentation and answer questions about your employment and background.

5. **Visa Issuance**: If approved, you will receive your visa and can make travel arrangements to the U.S.

Additional Considerations

- **Dual Intent**: Some visas, like the H-1B and L-1, allow for dual intent, meaning you can apply for a green card while on a temporary visa.

- **Dependents**: Many work visas allow you to bring your spouse and children under 21 years old. They may also be eligible for dependent visas, such as H-4 for H-1B dependents, which may allow them to work or study in the U.S.

This detailed guide should help you understand the various visa options and processes for working in the United States.

2 FINDING A JOB

Finding a Job in the U.S.

Job Search Strategies

Online Job Portals:

- **Indeed**: One of the largest job search engines, offering a wide range of job listings across various industries. You can filter jobs by location, salary, and company, and set up job alerts to receive notifications about new listings.

- **LinkedIn**: A professional networking site

that also serves as a powerful job search tool. You can connect with industry professionals, join relevant groups, and apply for jobs directly through the platform. LinkedIn also offers insights into company culture and employee reviews.

- **Glassdoor**: Known for its company reviews and salary information, Glassdoor also lists job openings. It's a great resource for researching potential employers and understanding what to expect in terms of compensation and work environment.

Networking:

- **Professional Networks**: Join industry-specific associations and groups, both online and offline. Attend conferences, seminars, and workshops to meet professionals in your field.

- **Alumni Networks**: Leverage connections from your alma mater. Many universities have alumni associations that offer networking events and job boards.

- **Social Media**: Use platforms like Twitter and Facebook to follow companies and industry leaders. Engage in discussions and share relevant content to increase your visibility.

Recruitment Agencies:

- **Specialized Agencies**: Some agencies focus on placing foreign workers in the U.S. They can help match your skills with job openings and guide you through the visa sponsorship process.

- **General Agencies**: Larger recruitment firms like Robert Half and ManpowerGroup offer a wide range of job opportunities across various industries.

Company Websites:

- **Direct Applications**: Visit the career pages of companies you are interested in. Many companies prefer candidates who apply directly through their websites. This can also give you a better understanding of the company's values and culture.

In-Demand Industries

Technology:

- **Software Development**: High demand for software engineers, developers, and programmers, especially in tech hubs like Silicon Valley, Seattle, and Austin.

- **Cybersecurity**: Increasing need for cybersecurity experts to protect against data breaches and cyber threats.

- **Data Science**: Growing demand for data scientists and analysts who can interpret complex data and provide actionable insights.

Healthcare:

- **Nursing**: Persistent shortage of nurses across the country, particularly in urban hospitals and healthcare facilities.

- **Medical Research**: Opportunities in pharmaceutical companies, research institutions, and universities.

- **Healthcare Administration**: Demand for healthcare managers and administrators to oversee operations in hospitals, clinics, and other healthcare facilities.

Engineering:

- **Civil Engineering**: Opportunities in construction, infrastructure projects, and urban development.

- **Mechanical Engineering**: Demand in industries such as automotive, aerospace, and manufacturing.

- **Electrical Engineering**: Opportunities in technology, telecommunications, and energy sectors.

Finance:

- **Accounting**: Need for accountants in public accounting firms, corporations, and government agencies.

- **Financial Analysis**: Demand for financial analysts in investment firms, banks, and corporations.

- **Investment Banking**: Opportunities in major financial centers like New York and Chicago, focusing on mergers and acquisitions, capital raising, and financial advisory services.

These strategies and industry insights should help you navigate the U.S. job market more effectively.

3 PREPARING YOUR APPLICATION

Resume and Cover Letter

Tailor Your Resume:

- **Highlight Relevant Experience and Skills**: Focus on the experiences and skills that are most relevant to the job you are applying for. Use specific examples and quantify your achievements where possible (e.g., "Increased sales by 20% over six months").

- **Use a Common U.S. Format**: U.S. resumes typically include sections such as Contact Information, Summary or Objective, Work Experience, Education, Skills, and Certifications. Avoid including personal information like age, marital status, or a photo.

- **Keywords**: Incorporate keywords from the job description into your resume. Many companies use Applicant Tracking Systems (ATS) to screen resumes, and using the right keywords can help ensure your resume gets noticed.

Write a Compelling Cover Letter:

- **Introduction**: Start with a strong opening that grabs the reader's attention. Mention the position you are applying for and how you found out about it.

- **Body**: Explain why you are interested in the position and how your background makes you a good fit. Highlight specific experiences and skills that align with the job requirements. Use this section to demonstrate your knowledge of the company and how you can contribute to its goals.

- **Conclusion**: End with a call to action, expressing your enthusiasm for the opportunity to discuss your application further. Thank the reader for their time and consideration.

Interview Preparation

Research the Company:

- **Company Culture and Values**: Visit the company's website and read about its mission, values, and culture. Look for information on the company's history, leadership, and recent news or achievements.

- **Products and Services**: Understand what the company offers and who its customers are. This knowledge will help you tailor your responses to show how you can add value.

- **Competitors and Industry Trends**: Familiarize yourself with the company's competitors and the latest trends in the industry. This can help you demonstrate your industry knowledge during the interview.

Practice Common Interview Questions:

- **Behavioral Questions**: Be prepared to answer questions about how you have handled specific situations in the past. Use the STAR method (Situation, Task, Action, Result) to structure your responses.

    o Example: "Tell me about a time when you faced a challenging project. How did you handle it?"

- **Technical Questions**: Depending on the role, you may be asked questions to assess your technical skills and knowledge. Review the key concepts and practices relevant to your field.

    o Example: "Explain how you would approach debugging a complex software issue."

- **General Questions**: Be ready to discuss your background, strengths, weaknesses, and career goals.

    o Example: "Why do you want to work for our company?"

Professional Attire:

- **Dress Code**: Research the company's dress code and industry standards. For most professional roles, business attire is appropriate. This typically means a suit and tie for men and a suit or professional dress for women.

- **Grooming and Presentation**: Ensure that your clothes are clean and well-fitted. Pay attention to grooming, such as neat hair and minimal, professional makeup. Avoid excessive jewelry or accessories.

By following these detailed steps, you can create a strong application

4 VISA APPLICATION PROCESS

Navigating the Visa Application Process

Employer Sponsorship

Key Points:

- **Job Offer**: Most work visas require a job offer from a U.S. employer who will sponsor your visa application.

- **Petition Filing**: The employer must file a petition with the U.S. Citizenship and Immigration Services (USCIS) on your behalf.

Application Steps

1. **Petition Approval**:

    - **Form I-129**: For nonimmigrant workers, the employer files Form I-129, Petition for a Nonimmigrant Worker, with USCIS. This form includes details about the job, the employee, and the employer.
2.
    - **Supporting Documents**: The petition must be accompanied by supporting documents, such as the job offer letter, proof of the employer's ability to pay the offered wage, and evidence of the employee's qualifications.
3.
    - **Processing Time**: USCIS processing times can vary. Premium processing is available for certain visa categories, which expedites the process for an additional fee.

4. **Visa Application**:

    - **Approval Notice**: Once the petition is approved, USCIS will send an approval notice (Form I-797) to the employer and the employee.
5.
    - **DS-160 Form**: The employee must complete the DS-160, Online Nonimmigrant Visa Application form. This form collects personal, travel, and employment information.
6.
    - **Application Fee**: Pay the non-refundable visa application fee. The amount varies depending on the visa type.
    -
7. **Interview**:

    - **Scheduling**: Schedule an interview at a U.S. embassy or consulate in your home country. Wait times for interview appointments can vary, so it's advisable to schedule early.

    - **Required Documents**: Gather the necessary documents for the interview, including:

- Passport valid for travel to the U.S.
- Confirmation page of the DS-160 form
- Receipt of visa application fee payment
- Form I-797 approval notice
- Job offer letter
- Educational and professional certificates
- Financial evidence (if applicable)

- **Interview Process**: During the interview, a consular officer will ask questions about your employment, background, and intentions in the U.S. Be honest and clear in your responses. The officer will review your documents and assess your eligibility based on U.S. visa regulations.

8. **Visa Issuance**:

    o **Processing Time**: After the interview, your visa application will be processed. Processing times can vary depending on the visa category and individual circumstances.

    o **Visa Collection**: If approved, you will be informed about when and how to collect your visa and passport. Some embassies and consulates offer courier services to deliver your documents.

Additional Tips for a Smooth Application Process

- **Check Eligibility**: Ensure you meet the eligibility criteria for the visa category you are applying for.

- **Prepare Thoroughly**: Have all your documents and information ready before your interview to avoid delays.

- **Understand Visa Restrictions**: Know the conditions and stay duration of your visa to ensure compliance with U.S. immigration laws.

Navigating the U.S. visa application process can be complex, but with careful preparation and a clear understanding of the steps involved, you can increase your chances of a successful application and a smooth journey to the United States

5 WORK CULTURE

Understanding U.S. Work Culture

Workplace Etiquette

Punctuality:

- **Importance:** Being on time is highly valued in the U.S. workplace. It demonstrates respect for others' time and a commitment to your responsibilities.

- **Tips:** Aim to arrive a few minutes early for meetings and appointments. If you anticipate being late, inform the relevant parties as soon as possible.

Communication:

- **Style:** Clear and direct communication is important. Americans appreciate straightforwardness and brevity. While politeness is valued, getting to the point quickly is often preferred.

- **Feedback:** Be open to receiving and giving feedback. Constructive criticism is a common part of professional development. It's important to accept feedback positively and use it to improve your performance.

- **Non-Verbal Cues:** Pay attention to body language and facial expressions. Maintaining eye contact is generally seen as a sign of confidence and honesty.

Professionalism:

- **Behavior:** Maintain a professional demeanor at all times. This includes being respectful, courteous, and cooperative with colleagues and supervisors.

- **Dress Code:** Dress appropriately for your industry and company culture. In more formal environments, business attire such as suits and ties for men and professional dresses or suits for women are expected. In more casual settings, business casual attire may be acceptable.

Work-Life Balance

Vacation and Leave:

- **Policies:** Understand your company's policies on vacation, sick leave, and other benefits. The U.S. does not have a federally mandated vacation policy, so benefits can vary widely between employers.

- **Paid Time Off (PTO):** Most companies offer between 10 to 15 days of PTO annually, in addition to public holidays. Some companies also offer additional leave for personal or family emergencies.

- **Sick Leave:** Policies on sick leave can vary. Some companies offer a set number of sick days, while others may provide flexible or unlimited sick leave.

Work Hours:

- **Typical Hours:** The standard workday is typically from 9 AM to 5 PM, but this can vary by industry and company. Some sectors, like finance and tech, may have longer hours, especially for senior roles.

- **Flexibility:** Many companies are increasingly offering flexible work hours and remote work options. This can help employees balance their professional and personal lives more effectively.

- **Overtime:** Be aware of your company's policies on overtime. Some positions may require additional hours beyond the standard workweek, and compensation for overtime can vary.

Balancing Professional and Personal Life:

- **Time Management:** Effective time management is crucial for maintaining a healthy work-life balance. Prioritize tasks and set boundaries to ensure you have time for personal activities and relaxation.

- **Wellness Programs:** Many companies offer wellness programs that include gym memberships, mental health resources, and other benefits to support employees' well-being.

- **Family-Friendly Policies:** Look for employers that offer family-friendly policies, such as parental leave, childcare support, and flexible working arrangements.

Understanding and adapting to U.S. work culture can significantly enhance your professional experience and help you succeed in your career.

6 LEGAL AND FINANCIAL

Legal and Financial Considerations

Social Security Number (SSN)

Importance of SSN:

- **Requirement**: You will need a Social Security Number (SSN) to work in the U.S. It is used to report your wages to the government and to determine your eligibility for Social Security benefits.

- **Application Process**: Your employer will assist you in applying for an SSN. You can apply for an SSN by completing Form SS-5, Application for a Social Security Card, and submitting it to the Social Security Administration (SSA) along with the required documentation.

Required Documents:

- **Proof of Identity**: Valid passport and visa.

- **Proof of Employment Authorization**: Employment Authorization Document (EAD) or a work visa.

- **Proof of Age**: Birth certificate or passport.

Application Steps:

1. **Complete Form SS-5**: Fill out the application form available on the SSA website or at a local SSA office.

2. **Submit Documents**: Provide the necessary documents to prove your identity, work authorization, and age.

3. **Receive SSN**: Once your application is processed, you will receive your SSN card by mail. This process typically takes about two weeks.

Taxes

Understanding Tax Obligations:

- **Federal Taxes**: All employees in the U.S. are subject to federal income tax. The amount withheld from your paycheck depends on your income level and the information you provide on Form W-4.

- **State and Local Taxes**: In addition to federal taxes, you may also be subject to state and local taxes, which vary depending on where you live and work.

- **Social Security and Medicare Taxes**: These are payroll taxes that fund Social Security and Medicare programs. Both you and your employer contribute to these taxes.

Filing Taxes:

- **Annual Tax Return**: You must file an annual tax return with the Internal Revenue Service (IRS) and, if applicable, with your state tax agency. The deadline for filing federal tax returns is typically April 15th.

- **Tax Treaties**: Some countries have tax treaties with the U.S. that may reduce or eliminate your tax liability. Check if your home country has such a treaty with the U.S.

- **Consult a Tax Professional**: Consider consulting a tax professional to ensure you understand your tax obligations and take advantage of any applicable deductions or credits.

Employment Rights

Minimum Wage Laws:

- **Federal Minimum Wage**: The federal minimum wage is $7.25 per hour, but many states and cities have higher minimum wages. Ensure you are aware of the minimum wage laws in your area.

- **Overtime Pay**: Non-exempt employees are entitled to overtime pay at a rate of 1.5 times their regular pay for hours worked over 40 in a workweek.

Workplace Safety:

- **Occupational Safety and Health Administration (OSHA)**: OSHA sets and enforces standards to ensure safe and healthy working conditions. Employers are required to provide a workplace free from recognized hazards.

- **Rights**: You have the right to report unsafe working conditions without fear of retaliation. OSHA provides resources and support for workers to understand their rights and report violations.

Anti-Discrimination Protections:

- **Equal Employment Opportunity Commission (EEOC)**: The EEOC enforces laws that prohibit discrimination based on race, color, religion, sex, national origin, age, disability, or genetic information.

- **Rights**: You have the right to a workplace free from discrimination and harassment. If you believe you have been discriminated against, you can file a complaint with the EEOC.

Understanding these legal and financial considerations will help you navigate your employment in the U.S.

7 SETTLING IN THE U.S.

Housing

Research Housing Options:

- **Websites**: Use websites like Zillow, Craigslist, and Realtor.com to explore housing options. These platforms allow you to filter by price, location, and type of housing (e.g., apartments, houses).

- **Neighborhood Research**: Research neighborhoods to find one that suits your lifestyle and budget. Consider factors such as proximity to work, schools, public transportation, and amenities.

- **Rental Agreements**: Understand the terms of rental agreements, including lease duration, security deposits, and maintenance responsibilities. It's common to sign a lease for one year, but shorter or longer terms may be available.

Costs:

- **Rent**: Rent prices vary widely depending on the city and neighborhood. Major cities like New York, San Francisco, and Los Angeles tend to have higher rents compared to smaller cities and rural areas.

- **Utilities**: In addition to rent, you may need to budget for utilities such as electricity, water, gas, and internet. Some rentals include certain utilities in the rent, so clarify this with your landlord.

Healthcare

Understanding the Healthcare System:

- **Private Healthcare**: The U.S. primarily relies on private healthcare providers. Health insurance is essential to cover medical expenses, as healthcare costs can be very high.

- **Health Insurance**: Obtain health insurance through your employer, a private insurer, or the Health Insurance Marketplace (Healthcare.gov). Employer-sponsored insurance is common and often more affordable.

- **Types of Plans**: Familiarize yourself with different types of health insurance plans, such as Health Maintenance Organizations (HMOs), Preferred Provider Organizations (PPOs), and High-Deductible Health Plans (HDHPs). Each has different coverage options and costs.

Finding Healthcare Providers:

- **Primary Care Physicians**: Establish a relationship with a primary care physician (PCP) for routine check-ups and non-emergency medical needs.

- **Specialists**: If you need specialized care, your PCP can refer you to a specialist. Ensure that the specialist is covered by your insurance plan.

Transportation

Public Transportation:

- **Options**: Major cities often have extensive public transportation systems, including buses, subways, and trains. Research the options available in your area.

- **Costs**: Public transportation costs vary by city. Monthly passes can be a cost-effective option if you plan to use public transit regularly.

Driving:

- **Car Ownership**: In areas with limited public transportation, owning a car may be necessary. Consider the costs of purchasing, insuring, and maintaining a vehicle.

- **Driver's License**: You will need a valid driver's license to drive in the U.S. If you have a foreign license, you may need to obtain a U.S. license. Check the requirements in your state.

Community and Support

Connecting with Local Communities:

- **Expatriate Groups**: Join local expatriate groups and online forums to connect with others who have moved to the U.S. These groups can provide valuable support and advice.

- **Cultural Organizations**: Participate in cultural organizations and events to meet people and learn more about your new community.

Support Services:

- **Local Resources**: Many cities offer resources for newcomers, such as community centers, libraries, and non-profit organizations that provide assistance with housing, employment, and legal matters.

- **Volunteering**: Volunteering is a great way to get involved in your community, meet new people, and gain a sense of belonging.

Settling into a new country can be challenging, but with the right resources and support, you can make a smooth transition to life in the U

Visit - Arthurcrandon.co.uk - for More Titles

Retirement to the Philippines
K1 Fiance visa to the U.S. – Fast Track
Secrets to buying Condos in the Philippines
Buying Land in the Philippines
Annulment in the Philippines
Breaking free from a bad marriage
Get a visit visa to America First time
Marriage in the Philippines
Get a visit visa to the United Kingdom
Ghosts, Spectres, and folklore in the Philippines
Retiring to Spain – a Comprehensive Guide
Spousal Visa to America
Spousal visa to the United Kingdom
Working in the UK

ABOUT THE AUTHOR

Arthur Crandon is a retired lawyer and a prolific writer. Hi is British and grew up in a rural community in Somerset. He has lived in England, Wales, Hong Kong and the Philippines and now spends most of his time in the Philippines with his Visayan wife and their son.

He loves to hear from anyone who has anything to do with the Philippines – you can email him anytime on:

ac@arthurcrandon.co.uk

www.ingramcontent.com/pod-product-compliance
Lightning Source LLC
Chambersburg PA
CBHW030053230526
45471CB00003B/1075